Abstract

The purpose of this study is to find out reasons or obstacles to explain why Vietnam has no PR association until now though other Association of South East Asian Nations (ASEAN) have their own once 40 to 50 years ago. The study also identifies challenges which PR practitioners in Vietnam are facing up in their works and if they need a PR professional organisation to support them to enhance their career development or not. Finally, the study shows what the PR professional organization is expected to contribute to the PR industry and business environment of Vietnam, especially when the Association of South East Asian Nations (AEC) is established in the end of 2015.

The methods used to research information are online survey with sample size of 100 PR practitioners and in-dept interview with 08 established and reputable practitioners. The study results showed that all PR practitioners agree the PR professional organisation (or PR association) could help them to solve their challenges. They think this organization could support them to "widen their network and open connections with other practitioners", "provide them useful training course" and "celebrate PR seminar to help their BOD understand about PR role".

Besides, agency practitioners expect this PR professional organization to become a force to fight against clients' negative requests because it set up code of conduct for the whole PR industry, and the benchmark of fees, including idea fee, proposal fee, consulting fee to protect practitioners' intellectual property.

However, it is not easy to establish the PR association in Vietnam. They explain that there is still not PR association in Vietnam because practitioners have not been able to be gathered due to lack of the qualified advocacy/proponent, benefit conflict and no commitment of contribution of time and financial resources. They agree that government should be the advocacy to establish PR association to overcome these issues.

In conclusion, PR industry in Vietnam is in its early dawn so it might take long time to have the PR association. However, the researcher hopes that this study could contribute a helpful voice to alert about the need of a PR professional organisation (or PR association) in Vietnam. It is hoped that Vietnam will be able to shape its way to give birth of an excellent and professional PR organisation in future.

About author

Mr. Le Tran Bao Phuong is known as one of the leading experts in Public Relations in Vietnam.

He got his Master of Communication from the University of Stirling (UK), and has assumed the position of communications counselor for several major labels and brands (such as GlaxoSmithKline, Ajinomoto VN, Kimberly Clark, ISN (US), Gibbs & Soell, Mead Johnson Nutrition, Study Group International, Rosatom, Vietrade, etc). He also gives lectures on public relations at the major universities.

With years working in the field of PR communication, he has conducted many specialized studies, notably the "Secret Power" book about PR market which is highly received.

With the success of this book, he has become one of the prestigious experts that entrepreneurs consult and listen to on creating communication strategy and the application of public relations in Vietnam.

Table of content

Acknowledgement

I would like to thank to my UK tutor **Dr. Indrani Lahiri** as well as my Vietnamese tutor **Ms. Khong Loan** who gave me the golden support to finish this meaningful study on the topic "Public Relations and the need to form a professional organisation in Vietnam".

This study is the first ever research which explores about the persistent problem of PR industry in Vietnam (a communist country) and provides suggestions to solve out the problem in trend of regional integration and internationalization. There is no public relations study in Vietnam has ever undertaken this mission before.

List of table

List of acronyms

Association of South East Asian Nations (ASEAN)

ASEAN Economic Community (AEC)

Public Relations (PR)

Managing Director (MD)

London School of Public Relations (LSPR)

Thailand Public Relations Association (TPRA)

Institute of Public Relations of Singapore (IPRS)

Public Relations Society of the Philippines (PRSP)

Institute of Public Relations Malaysia (IPRM)

Board of Director (BOD)

CHAPTER 1

INTRODUCTION

At present, it is much urgent for Vietnam because it does not have public relations association though other Association of South East Asian Nations (ASEAN) such as Indonesia, Malaysia, Singapore, Thailand, Philippine, have their own one half of a century ago. If there were a PR association in Vietnam, PR practitioners and business organisations would gain much benefit from it. PR practitioners would have their "home" to open their network and career development opportunities, while business organisations could achieve their business goals through effective and ethic PR practices. Moreover, they could have a PR association to claim for and solve out dirty communication activities of their competitors.

Furthermore, the PR professional organisation (or PR association) should be the bridge among PR practitioners, business organisations and the government. Business organisations' voice and PR practitioners' voice could be transferred to government through PR association and vice versa. It makes the PR industry and the business environment develop healthier and stronger especially when AEC is established. PR association should also be a trusted unit to help business enterprises in promoting brands within ASEAN and the world.

There has been no official explanation for this big concern up to now though the researcher believes that many PR practitioners knows the reason why. Therefore, the purpose of this study is to find out reasons to explain why Vietnam has no PR association until now. The study also identifies challenges which PR practitioners in Vietnam are facing up in their works and if they need a PR professional organisation to support them to enhance their career development or not. Finally, the study shows what the PR professional organization is expected to contribute to the PR industry and business environment of Vietnam, especially when the Association of South East Asian Nations (AEC) is established in the end of 2015.

According to website of ASEAN (2014), AEC envisages the following key characteristics: (a) a single market and production base, (b) a highly competitive economic region, (c) a region of equitable economic development, and (d) a region fully integrated into the global economy. That includes the implementation of the objectives of the group's economic pillar to transform the region into a single, production-based market. This process also covers aspects of an ASEAN socio-cultural community which can encourage cultural and people-to-people contact across borders.

AEC is going to be established in 2015 which aims to improve the free flow of goods, services, investment and labour throughout the region (Vietnam +, 2014) and to allow people to earn benefits from building a common community (Vita A.D. Busyra, 2014). Particularly, the AEC could create 14 million new jobs and increase overall growth by 7.1% by 2025 (ILO, 2014).

By 2015, the Southeast Asia Economic Community will also become a common market and then competition among nations will be extremely fierce. This put PR practitioners of nations into high rival when the rotation of PR professionals among nations is much more open. Thus, Ms Prita Kemal Gani, a founder of PR ASEAN network (2014) said: *'The preparedness of PR professionals in the various countries is vital to increasing awareness and self-confidence toward the dynamic change of world demand for PR services'* (in Busyra, 2014).

However, Vietnam has no PR associations while other ASEAN have their own one for near a half of a century ago. This issue will cause negative affects to both Vietnamese enterprises and PR practitioners as mentioned above. Therefore, the researcher proposes Vietnam should have the PR professional organisation to deal with these matters. So, this research contributes toward the scope of the foundation of PR association in Vietnam. It looks into the challenges, needs and expectations within the PR practitioner community in Vietnam.

This study is related to public relations. So, the researcher will examine books, journals, reports and any official information source about public relations in the world, in ASEAN and in Vietnam to serve for this study.

2. Problem statement:

The AEC is going to be established at the end of 2015. So, the researcher highlights that without having supports from any professional organisation, Vietnamese enterprises will face up challenges when they promote their goods in common market. In addition, Vietnamese PR practitioners will lose opportunities and supports for their career development. The issue becomes urgent day by day.

This study will provide social contribution because it is the first ever study which explores about the persistent problem of PR industry in Vietnam and provides suggestions to solve out the problem in trend of regional integration and internationalization. No public relations study in Vietnam has ever undertaken this mission before.

About its content, in the first chapter, the researcher introduces the structure and content of the research. In the second chapter, the researcher reviews theories of public relations in the world, in ASEAN and in Vietnam. In details, it includes definition of PR, its origin, its development status and representative PR associations around these areas. In the third chapter, the researcher presents the research questions and shares in details the research methodology and field experiences. In the fourth chapter, the researcher answers each research question by generating raw data of online survey and in-dept interview. Moreover, he analyzes and compares findings between survey method and interview method to discover and discuss deeper explanation about the situation. This allows the researcher to provide suggestion to public relations in Vietnam. The final chapter will present a list of answers for each researcher questions and suggestion for further study.

In the following chapter Literature review, the researcher reviews the theories of public relations in the world, in ASEAN and in Vietnam to explain his understandings about the research topic.

CHAPTER 2

LITERATURE REVIEW

This chapter looks into the PR definitions, origin, development status and representative PR associations around the world, in ASEAN and in Vietnam. This contributes to understand overall pictures of public relations perceptions and PR associations around the world.

According to Bao Phuong (2014), communication is an ever-changing field adapting to the changing of political, economic situation and cultural development at every country (p. 85). Culture is also an ever-changing field, while communication and culture are influenced each other" (Hall, 1981; Hofstede, 1980; Sriramesh, 2007). PR is one of the communication activities. Thus, PR varies in different cultures and in different territory.

Daniel Lerner (1973) suggests that mass communication is the main contributing factor in helping people to be exposed to many different ideas and public affairs of society. Based on Lerner's argument, in *The Secret Power* (Le Tran Bao Phuong, pp. 64-82), the author highlighted that PR has the ability to create harmony in society and help to enhance empathy in the crowd. In PR, empathy in society is created because the crowd may be exposed to many different ideas and knows the social issues through two-way communication which is supported by the mass media. The crowd becomes more empathetic, more understanding, more tolerant and more harmonious.

PR has also created the indirect experiences by spreading and disseminating of testimonials, comments, evaluations and reviews through mass media, social media, forums, etc. The buying mechanism of the crowd relies heavily on these indirect experiences because none of us know everything. We need to learn from others' experiences to solve our problems. We need indirect experiences. This mechanism projects the important role of PR in modern society (Le, 2014, pp. 90-93). Thus, this chapter reviews literatures on PR, the root of PR, PR development status and representative PR associations in the world, in ASEAN and in Vietnam.

PR in the world

The origin of PR

Curtin and Gaither (2007) argued that the using of PR techniques has arised from the civilization of ancient Egypt about 3500 years ago. Evidently, the first female pharaoh Hatshepsut of Egypt (1508-1458 BC) is one of the most powerful female monarch in the history of the ancient world, even though the female king ruling the Egypt was very rare. That Hatshepsut's rule lasted more than 20 years (about 1479-1458 BC) and was the longest reign compared to those of other

Queens of ancient Egypt. Hatshepsut was also admired the ability to skillfully achieve the passionate support from the crowd (Curtin and Gaither, 2007, pp. 6 - 10).

In fact, at that time, there was no PR firm for Hatshepsut to hire to build up her personal image in the hearts of the people, but she was surrounded by the real and strategic Public Relations Adviser. They advised Hatshepsut on how to use public relations techniques to protect and maintain her crown. They advised her to use images and symbols of kingship to represent the power of the real Pharaoh. They helped her to confirm her status of a supreme ruler rather than a "great wife of the King". They advised her on how to govern the crowd according to the character of a power king to suit the Egypt patriarchal society. So, the root of public relations is as old as the civilization of ancient Egypt (Curtin and Gaither, 2007, pp. 6 - 10).

According Cornelissen (2009: 14-32), in the 19th century, PR was born. This was a flourishing time for the industrial revolution in Britain and America. The industrial conglomerates hired journalists, propagandist and the press agent to implement communication campaigns to serve their purpose. At that time, these communicators often exaggerated and misled matters because the majority of people were gullible. But until the early of the 20th century, this bad communication practice ended when the journalist started to investigate in and expose scandals involving financial crime and corruption. In US this time, journalists raised awareness of the public about unethical business operations. So, many large organisations hired other journalists as their spokespersons to respond to allegation and spread positive information widely to gain the support of the crowd.

Between 1920-1930, due to the economic reforms in the United State, United Kingdom and skepticism in the public for large organisations increasing, these large organisations need the help of communicators more frequently. Therefore, they hired communication experts to do internal and external communications strategically. The organisation has used PR to make them become closer to the concerns of the public. PR has started operating its development since that time (Cornelissen, 2014, pp. 14-32).

As defined by the World Assembly of Public Relations Associations in 1978, 'Public relations is the art and social science of analysing trends, predicting their consequences, counselling organisational leaders and implementing planned programmes of action which will serve both the organisations and the public interest' (Wilcox et al. 2003: 6). This definition emphasizes both on the art and planning of PR in implementation. It has also affirmed the moral of this job which should not neglect the interests of the public.

As defined by The Chartered Institute of Public Relations (CIPR) in 2014, 'Public Relations is about reputation - the result of what you do, what you say and what others say about you. Public Relations is the discipline which looks after reputation, with the aim of earning understanding and support and influencing opinion and behaviour. It is the planned and sustained effort to establish and maintain goodwill and mutual understanding between an organisation and its publics'. This definition emphasizes the role of PR as an indispensable communication activity of an organisation. PR is not advertising.

The PRSA (1982) formally adopted a definition of PR as 'Public relations help an organisation and its publics adapt mutually to each other'. And in 2012, PRSA initiated a crowdsourcing campaign that produced the following definition "Public relations is a strategic communication process that builds mutually beneficial relationships between organisations and their publics." In summary, there are plenty of definitions about PR in the world because it is perceived differently in cultures and countries.

The status of PR in the world

The rapid development of the Internet and satellite TV has spread strongly information about goods and products / services throughout the world (Sriramesh & Vercic, 2003). In addition, the global demand for goods and services has increased significantly and people have become free in democracy, so they can buy anything at anywhere, in any country. This has led to the significant increase in the global suppliers for goods and services. Moreover, countries in Africa, Asia, the Middle East, Eastern Europe and Latin America have become, or will soon become, the major centers of both goods production and consumption. This requires enterprises of these countries to trade and communicate with the global audience to do sales.

Last but not least, the formation of the multinational trading block such as NAFTA, EU, ASEAN, APEC and ASEM has also contributed to shrink the global market and strengthen the interaction among organisations, among blocks and among the organisation and blocks together. These factors set out requirements that the PR practitioners should be the leader in managing the relationship and interaction between their organisations and the people of countries. This projects the important role of the PR.

According Sriramesh, K., & Vercic, D. (2003: 22-37), in the second half of the 20th century, democratization of the world forced organisations of all kinds to consider the greater importance of public relations and communication management. 85 countries (including 35% of the world population) was classified by Freedom House (2000) as liberal democracies. This process of democratization reached crescendo in the 1990s when the former Soviet Union has embarked on the journey towards pluralism. As a result, the emerging democracies in the world have seen a significant growth in public communication, many of which will have to be managed by PR practitioners.

About the development of PR industry, in an interview in Davos Forum, Paul Holmes – the Founder and CEO of The Holmes Report (2010) shares: "I don't see a reason why PR shouldn't continue to expand. If we live in a world where information, transparency, democracy and freedom of choice continue to expand, then so will PR! Today the industry has to be involved in setting a policy rather than communicating it: that's a major part of building relationships with the public."

Moreover, on Youtube, Paul Holmes (2010) highlighted that PR industry is suffering the most frugal three issues which are: not good at recruiting the best talent; not good at research, and evaluation, measurement, ROI and has not good at building its own image and reputation. PR industry needs to get much better at those issues in the global view.

PR associations in the world

Following years of development, there are many PR professional organisations in the world like the Public Relations Society of America (PRSA) in United State, Chartered Institute of Public Relations (CIPR) in United Kingdom. These organisations contribute much to their countries. For example, the PRSA, which was founded in 1947, provides professional development, sets standards of excellence and upholds principles of ethics for its members and aim to advocate for greater understanding and adoption of public relations services (PRSA website, 2014). Meanwhile, CIPR is a professional body in the United Kingdom that was founded in 1948. This association provides its members with education, updated research and a code of conduct to enhance their professionalism (CIPR website, 2014).

PR in ASEAN

Sriramesh and Vercic (2003) argued that the political system, culture and media (media control, media outreach and media access) are the three most important environmental factors that affect the nature of public relations practices in different cultures. So, due to differences in political systems and media, the nature of public relations in Asian countries is different from those in Western countries.

Wu (2005) explains that while PR has been mainly used as a business tool for organisations in the United State, it is used as a political tool for some Asian governments as a nation-building tool. Van Leuven (1996), who studied about PR practice in Southeast Asia, argued that PR has been used by the government of Malaysia and Singapore as a tool for national development.

According Haque (2004) in most Asian countries, the role of public relations practitioners have been contributing to the development of communication. In this form, the government plays a dominant role as they leverage all media and communication resources in their countries to achieve the economic and social objectives. In 1960, a campaign called "Lungs for Singapore" was launched to create a green environment in Singapore (Haque, 2004, pp. 341 – 362). The government has also implemented a "Speak Mandarin" campaign to encourage people to use of Mandarin to promote trade and do commercial with China (Haque, 2004, pp. 341 – 362). Another example, in 2007, Vietnam government launched the campaign called "Please wear helmet" to raise community awareness about the importance of wearing a helmet and to aim at reducing casualties caused by traffic accidents. Haque (2004) concluded that, "in most of the Asian countries that are less developed or are developing, public relations is only part of government development programs requiring large media campaign to mobilizing people to participate in a variety of socio-economic programs to uplift the society "(p. 351).

The status of PR in ASEAN

Last June 2014, the ASEAN PR Network (APRN), a non-profit organisation, was formally launched by the London School of Public Relations (LSPR) in Jakarta. PR professionals from Vietnam, Indonesia, Singapore, Malaysia, Thailand, Vietnam and the Philippines made the commitment to bolster networking capabilities, partnerships, relationships, and commonness among the PR community in the ASEAN arena ahead of the implementation of the regional economic community by the end of 2015. (Bong R. Osorio, 2014).

According to these PR professionals at APRN Conference in June 2014, PR is still an unclear concept to the Asia community; PR is being accused of "dark arts" in China, and businesses have not recognized PR as the essential activities. PR practitioners have not yet to demonstrate how they could help businesses achieve business goals. So, according to Bong R. Osorio (2014): "the establishment of the APRN was a perfect opportunity for people to get to know each other better in terms of professional standards, competencies, and individual perspectives about public relations". It is the perfect opportunity for PR in Asia.

Ms Prita Kemal Gani enthused at the APRN that: "We have gathered to talk about the benchmark associated with ethics, skills and knowledge of public relations, and we can definitely learn from the best practices of professionals and educators around the region". She stated that the communication leaders of the 10 ASEAN countries will support the birth of the AEC and PR will be a major and important component as open borders open. She also highlighted that it is the high time for 10 ASEAN PR professional associations of 10 countries to cooperate together to support the AEC.

PR associations in ASEAN

However, not all ASEAN has PR professional associations. Although most of ASEAN has established their own PR associations to contribute to the nation's growth 40 - 50 years ago, Vietnam has no one. For example, Thailand has set up the Thailand Public Relations Association (TPRA) since 1970s to contribute to Thailand's communication development, image, social and economic advancement; Singapore has established the Institute of Public Relations of Singapore (IPRS) in 1970 to establish growth for Singapore's PR industry, Philippines has formed the Public Relations Society of the Philippines (PRSP) in 1957 to become the country's premier organisation for public relations professionals; Malaysia has founded the Institute of Public Relations Malaysia (IPRM) in 1962 to contribute positively to the nation's continuous growth and development in all spheres of human endeavors. That Vietnam has no PR professional association in a long time is the big concern, but before going to research to find out the answer, this study analyzes about the current situation of PR in Vietnam.

PR in Vietnam

The origin of PR in Vietnam

There are many books, studies that have discussed about the international PR and PR in Asia, but there are few works that mention about the PR situation in Vietnam. In reality, there are only three remarkable authors. They are Bruce C. Mckinney, Hang Dinh and Hanh Nguyen.

Generally, while Bruce recounts his personal observations of the level of PR development in Vietnam from 1999-2006, Hang Dinh focused on presenting the role of PR in business, in government. She argued that PR is the potential and bright career. Meanwhile, Hanh Nguyen projects her research findings about the public understandings about PR functions, PR practitioners' roles and important skills for PR practitioners in Vietnam.

In particular, Bruce C. Mckinney (1999) wrote that "public relations is in its infancy in Vietnam" (p. 23). Then, in 2006, when he returned to Vietnam, he found out that PR in Vietnam had not progressed very far (McKinney, 2006). With the population of over 80 million, there were just nine PR agencies in Ho Chi Minh City and two in Hanoi. It seems to be difficult this time to know the exact number of PR agencies and the number of PR practitioners in Vietnam because there has not had any official professional organisation like the Chartered Institute of Public Relations (CIPR) or Public Relations Society of America (PRSA) in Vietnam.

According to Hang Dinh (2010), PR began in Vietnam in the 90s and it has been considered one of the most popular careers in Vietnam thanks to its activeness, creativity and high income. But she also highlighted that in Vietnam, even a communication manager or PR manager would take the execution role rather than the strategic planning role. They often execute the available plans proposed by the Board of Directors because most of them are young and lack of experiences. It is easy to understand because PR practice in Vietnam is in its early dawn without any law or standardization, she concluded.

According to her research, Hanh Nguyen found that the importance of public relations is generally recognized in Vietnamese organisations. Moreover, public relations practitioners are well respected in their organisations. Today, with all of these developments, it can be gathered that public relations in Vietnam is no longer in its infancy. Public relations practitioners in Vietnam perform communication technician roles rather than strategic management roles.

The status of PR in Vietnam

According to Vietnamnews (2014), "the public relations industry in Viet Nam has huge potential to develop, but a legal framework and code of practice are needed to ensure healthy development of the industry, according to experts". The increase in foreign-invested enterprises and the need to build a strong brand image among local and foreign enterprises in the country have offered a great opportunity for the PR industry in Vietnam. But a lack of specific regulations on the operation of PR companies has led to the uncontrolled proliferation of companies with such unhealthy practices.

Le Thu Quyen (2014), general director of Galaxy Communications, said to Vietnamnews that the PR industry in Vietnam has faced up challenges, such as unhealthy competition and violations of intellectual property rights, affecting its industry reputation. With increased demand for PR services, PR firms have mushroomed in recent years. She emphasizes that: "Many of them have not focused on the development of their service quality, but conducted unhealthy practices by lowering prices to win contracts". Once again, Nguyen Thanh Dao (2014), general secretary of the HCM City Advertising Association, said that other challenge of PR industry in Vietnam is the lack of good PR professionals (same as Paul Holmes' point of view). He also suggested that PR firms focus more on improving their PR professionals and exchanging experiences with international communication firms.

PR associations in Vietnam

Vietnam has no PR association though researches of three authors have shared important thinking about PR industry in Vietnam, such as Vietnam should have a PR professional organisation, a specific regulation, a legal framework, code of practice to ensure a healthy development of the industry as well as training programs to improve PR talents. Moreover, these three researchers have not answered effectively either questions about current challenges of PR practitioners in their work, the need of a PR professional organisation and the supports offered from this organisation that help PR practitioners as well as PR industry develop healthily. So, this research will answer these questions and brings continuity, contribution in addition to previous studies. In the third chapter, the researcher presents research questions and shares in details his research methodology, his implementation, what challenges he had faced up in the implement process and how he has conquered them effectively.

CHAPTER 3

METHODOLOGY

This is the unique study in Vietnam which discuss about the problem of the PR industry in trend of regional integration and internationalization. There have not been any similar study topics before. The study attempted to project the up-to-date picture of PR practice in Vietnam and helps to answer what challenges of Vietnamese PR practitioners in their work, if they need a PR professional organisation in Vietnam and what the supports offered from this organisation that could help them develop their career and contribute to the Vietnam PR industry.

As a result, this study will use survey method mainly to answer these following research questions:

Research Question 1.   What challenges PR practitioners in Vietnam are facing within their works?

Research Question 2.   How do they think to solve these challenges themselves?

Research Question 3.   How do they think a PR professional organisation can support to solve their problems?

Research Question 4.   How do they think a PR professional organisation can also contribute to the development of PR industry in Vietnam, especially when AEC is established?

Research Question 5.   How do they think they can contribute to this PR professional organisation?

The researcher acknowledges that studying about public relations in Vietnam with the participation is PR practitioners (not Marketing, Advertising, Communication, Creative practitioners) is very difficult. As McKinney (2008, p.48) noted that "finding actual public relations practitioners would be extremely difficult - they just aren't that many in Vietnam. Currently, most public relations in Vietnam tend to be out-sourced to public relations companies that tend to be directed by non-Vietnamese individuals". McKinney (2008) also noted that an online survey would most likely never be returned because people will not respond to our survey unless you are referred by someone they know.

According to Nghia Nguyen (1995), though surveys is a good method to provide researcher reliable findings, statistical number of issue in a wide range, it has it own limitation because it separates feedback of participants from the social context (p4). Thus, in this study the researcher conducts in-dept interview to gain better and more insightful information about public relations in Vietnam. So, it could answer more a big concern of why Vietnam has not has PR association as other ASEAN has one 40 - 50 years ago satisfactorily. The following sections will describe the subjects and procedures of each method.

Methods 1: Online survey

According to Stacks (2002), survey method has been the most common research methodology used in PR. He also advised four ways to collect data, such as via telephone, email, face-to-face and online. The researcher chooses online survey as the main method for this study because it is quick, less expensive and easy to get feedback with 100 participants. The researcher will send online survey to personal emails of 100 PR practitioners to collect their answers for the 5 research questions above (please see detailed survey questions in Appendix C & D).When they full-fill the form, their feedback will be transferred to researcher's email to be established the master data.

Sample

The sample is 100 PR practitioners who are from leading PR agencies in Vietnam and from business enterprises. This sample of 100 people is large enough to ensure trusted research findings. There are 3 sources that the researcher could collect PR practitioners' emails to do online survey.

The first one, I have collected their personal emails through career website (careerbuilder, vietnamwork), then encourage them to send back their fulfilled survey. The second one, for the PR practitioners (or informants) from PR agencies, I am authorized by nine Managing Directors (MDs) to collect their employees' emails to do this survey, because I am being the facilitator of PR network – a group of nine leading PR agencies in Vietnam (Aid, Biz-Eyes, AVC Edelman, Venus Communications, Galaxy Communications, Pioneer Communications, Vietgate Communications, TeamworkPR and T&A Ogilvy). The third one, for the informants from PR in-house, I can disseminate widely the questionnaire to earn for research feedback through two channels (my Linkedin account, PR club facebook fanpage)

Overcome predicted challenges of online survey method:

To have a list of 100 PR practitioners is not easy especially there is no PR association in Vietnam. Thus, the researcher has his own solution to overcome these challenges as below:

- For PR practitioners from agency, each MD sends me one staff to establish the executional team (9 staff). I have right to lead this team to run activities of PR network. Therefore, I can have each staff of each agency collect emails and follow up informants to send back the questionnaire.
- For PR practitioners from business organisations, I try to publicize questionnaire generally as much as possible through LinkedIn connection, personal facebook account, local PR fanpage and my website letranbaophuong.com.

Implementation of online survey

Challenges

Though the researcher has predicted and prepared well to overcome challenges to complete online survey effectively, there are lots of unfavorable incidents rised up in the progress of implementation unexpectedly. They make the list of PR practitioner and high survey return rate become something which is extremely difficult to achieve.

In details, when the researcher starts to get list of PR practitioner from every PR agency, the MDs suddenly become fear of this activities. They are afraid of their employees' contacts being collected. Then their employees could be enticed by a certain PR firms. They are worried of losing their talents especially it is the high time of running PR campaigns at the end of fiscal year 2014. This is reason why they turn their back and not support to deliver their PR list. The researcher has explained earnestly via email and phone to gain back their supports. As a result, one of nine PR agencies agrees to assist.

To compensate for the lack of emails which are expected to be provided by PR agencies, the researcher has spent too much effort to get email of each PR practitioner from the career websites (career builder, vietnamwork). These email addresses belong to PR practitioners. It is reliable because it is the email of those people who are looking for job and who they say they are. However, this collecting email activity has taken researchers a lot of efforts and time.

Besides, the wide spreading online survey generally (via LinkedIn connection, personal facebook account, local PR fanpage) brings a few responses. It is easy to understand because the researcher has acknowledged this situation by McKinney's notes (as mentioned above).

Outcome

As a result of big efforts, the researcher has been able to have a list of 100 PR practitioners. However, before sending online survey out to them, the researcher does not expect to earn the high response rate. It is the normal status of online survey about PR topics. As Wu & Taylor's (2003) said that Taiwanese public relations study reported a 44% return rate. Wu &Baah-Boakye's (2007) noted that Ghana public relations study had a 53% response rate while while Ken et al.'s (2006) study on Bosnia public relations reported a 38% response rate. It may be explained that it is essential to establish a relationship with someone before asking him to finish an online survey without any rewards.

For this study, the researcher has sent out 100 surveys and received back 53 respondents (53% return rate). There is no reward committed for participants to complete this survey. So, this return rate is good and acceptable compared to another PR studies.

Methods 2: In-depth Interview

Kvale (1996) emphasized that the interview research helps to "understand the world from the subjects' points of view, to unfold the meaning of people's experiences, to uncover their lived world prior to scientific explanations" (p. 8). In addition, Stacks (2002) explained that the advantage of in-depth interview was to allow researchers to understand the problem being researched as well as the interviewed participants. Furthermore, Nghia Nguyen (1995) said that qualitative research with in-depth interview provides researchers deeper detail of a particular issue (pp. 5-7). So, besides online survey, the researcher has connected and invited established and reputable PR professionals by participating in in-dept interview. Seven PR professionals have been contacted as listed below:

(hidden information)

Overcome predicted challenges of interview method:

It will be not easy to get approval of these reputable PR professionals for in-dept interview because they may be very busy in this period of time (the end of the year) or they may be on business travelling most of the time. The researcher expected to invite about three people to do in-dept interview.

To achieve this goal, besides having contact with MDs as an facilitator of PR Network, the researcher has Ms Khong Loan, Journalist of Forbes Vietnam (also as the Vietnamese tutor of Stirling) connect him with two people (number 6, 7 in the list above) and encourage these professionals to participate in his interview. After they give approval, the researcher will send them the covering letter (please see Appendix A) with clear purpose of the in-dept interview as well as the interview questions (please see Appendix B).

Knowing that MDs' schedule will be full of events in the end of the year, the researcher advise them to answer questions on word file and send back to him via email. Then, the researcher could call them after receiving their answer to make clear their points or adding some additional information (if any). It is also good for participants because it makes us feel comfortable and could solve out the differences of location and convenient time.

Implementation of in-dept interview:

The researcher has contacted PR professionals as listed above. Effectively, the researcher got approval of five people and has interviewed them. All of them were interviewed by face-to-face interview. The other two people prefer to share his/her opinions via telephone only because they are in different location (Ha Noi captial) when the researcher is in Ho Chi Minh city.

These five senior PR professionals have average over 10 year experiences. They have spent years in manager position from PR in-house to PR agency. So, their answers are very valuable to the study, especially when comparing their points to those of the PR practitioner community.

The outcome is good although two people disagree to join or not wish to participate in. One of them shares that he is not very knowledgeable in PR industry although he is strong at general communications and branding. Another people agree to help but then she keeps silent though she has confirmed to send her answer back and the researcher and Ms Khong Loan reminded her two times. She may be very busy. Finally, she sent back her answer to support the researcher.

About the confidentiality requirement committed with interviewees, the researcher is not allowed to name any individual or reveal any signal which could deduce participants who have given their views. All of these senior PR experts require the researcher to keep confidential their viewpoint due to information sensitiveness.

Data collection and data analysis

The responses of the online survey were collected in over two months. It is planned by the researcher, because to encourage and follow informants to finish the survey without any rewards must take time. As a result, 53 completed surveys were sent back among 100 surveys sent out. In next step, the data will be analyzed by the Statistical Package for the Social Sciences (SPSS, version 16) software to release findings and answer research questions mentioned in the study.

Regarding to semi-structured in-dept interview, it took the researcher two months to connect and collect information from interviewees. The interview questions were conducted with nine people. There were people who disagreed to participate for varied reasons. One shares that he is not very knowledgeable in PR industry. He is strong at general communications and brands. Another agrees to help but then she keeps silent about sending her answer back though the researcher reminds her two times. The last one kept silent and the researcher received no feedback.

There were five interviewees who agreed to participate in the interview. None of them agreed to answer questions in word file and send back because they are very busy at this time (end of fiscal year 2014). 50% of them (3 people) agree to do face-to-face interview while the rest 50% (3 people) agreed to share his/her opinions via telephone only.

After collecting answers from interviewees, the researcher has coded the transcripts and analysed the data. The interview data was used as the qualitative data source which helps to provide deeper explanation for the discussion.

In the next chapter, the researcher will answer each research question by generating raw data of online survey and in-dept interview in Results section. Moreover, in Analysis section, the researcher will analyze and compare findings between survey method and interview method to discover and discuss deeper explanation about the situation. This will allow the researcher to provide suggestion to solve out the persistent problem of public relations in Vietnam.

CHAPTER 4

RESULTS AND ANALYSIS

Respondent Analysis

There are a total of 100 surveys were sent to 100 PR practitioners via email. 53 surveys were sent back, achieving 53% respond rate. Gender of respondent (table 1) shows 22 respondents (42%) were male and 31 respondents (58%) were female. A total of 44 respondents (83%) worked in Ho Chi Minh City, 4 respondents (7.5%) worked in Ha Noi and the rest of 5 respondents (9.5%) indicated that they worked in another location.

Fifteen respondents (28.3%) worked for PR agency only while thirty-eight respondents (71.7%) have worked for both PR agency and corporation (in-house). When breakdown respondents by Age and Sex (table 3), the researcher records that the youngest respondents is male (age of 18-22) and the oldest respondent is female (age of 40-60).

The quantitative data (table 4) also revealed that the most of respondents has $1 - 5$ years of working experiences (71.7%) and $3 - 5$ years (26.4%) and the average year of working experience of total 53 PR practitioners is 3.73 years. The year of working experience is varied from less than 1 year to over 10 years. It is notable that in PR field, a person can achieve managerial position when he/she has $1 - 3$ years of working experience (table 4).

Moreover, 26 of 53 respondents (49%) self-indicating that they hold a managerial role while 27 of them (51%) identify that they do not hold at managerial position (table 5). Especially, 13 out of 31 female respondents (42%) self-identify that they are holding managerial role while 13 out of 22 male respondents (59%) self-identify their managerial position (table 6, table 1).

Study Results

This research contributes toward the scope of the foundation of PR association in Vietnam. It looks into the challenges, needs and expectations within the PR practitioner community in Vietnam. Thus, the survey includes 13 questionnaires that could help to explore opinions and experiences of PR practitioners about the matter. These questionnaires were designed by both multiple-choice questions and rating-scale questions. The rating-scale question is between with 1 being "very disagree" and with 5 being "totally agree". The researcher is going to show the results of each questionnaire to answer research questions.

Part 1: For in-house PR practitioners

1. What are your own challenges you are facing up with in your works?

For this question, respondents could choose multiple answers. The answers were divided into nine variables. They are named as "challenge1", "challenge2" and so on to "challenge8" (table 8).

Twenty-one of respondents' choices (25%) indicate that the lack of helpful relations (with journalist, vendor, expert, influencer, opinion leader) is one of challenges in their works (challenge 1). Seventeen of choices (17%) choose the lack of experience as one of the challenges of in-house PR practitioners (challenge 5). Fourteen of selection from practitioners (14%) raises that among their challenges in works is the lack of knowledge about the product / service / industry / business sector (challenge 4).

The lack of PR knowledge (challenge 2) and lack of specialized skills (writing, planning, managing risks and crisis, establishing relationship…) (challenge 3) were chosen by the eleven of choices (11%) from PR practitioners. Eight of choices (10%) considered lack of study and research materials (challenge 6) as their challenge in works while four of choices (5%) indicate that limitation of English communication (challenge 7) is their problem. There are two of selections of practitioners (2%) agree that limitation of employment information (challenge 8) is their own problem in their work. In addition, respondents added that their challenges in works are also the gap of PR standards between Vietnam and the world. They face difficulties when applying the PR practice of the world into Vietnam.

> *2. How do you think you could solve your own challenges yourself (question 1) and how you evaluate its effectiveness?*

For this question, the respondents are allowed to select multiple answers that are suitable for their opinion. The answers are broken down into six variables. They are named as "solution1", "solution2", and so on, to "solution5" (table 9). Additionally, respondents are also allowed to give their evaluation score of effectiveness to each of solution they chose (table 10).

Twenty-four of choices from practitioners (30%) answer that establishing new relationship through current connections (solution 1) is among of their plans to solve their own challenges. Their evaluation score of effectiveness of solution 1 is 3.81 which fell to the "agree" category. Twenty of practitioners' selection (25%) indicates that participating in seminars, networking events (solution 2) is one of ideas in their solution list. Their evaluation score of effectiveness of solution 2 is 3.53 which fell between the "neutral" and "agree" category.

Achieving the percentage of choice is 25%, searching further information in local and international magazine, newspaper and internet (solution 4) is chosen as among the way that PR practitioners use to solve their issue. Sixteen of choices (20%) state that participating in related training courses (solution 3) is one of solution of practitioners to enhance their weaknesses. The evaluation score of effectiveness of solution 3 and solution 4 is 3.56 and 3.53. They fell between the "neutral" and "agree" category. One choice (1%) from practitioners replied that searching career opportunities from head hunters, internet (solution 5) could help to solve their challenges in works. Its evaluation score of effectiveness is 2.46 which fell between the "disagree" and "neutral" category.

3. What are challenges from working environment you are facing up with in your works?

Similar to question 1 and 2, in the third questions, the respondents are also allowed to choose multiple answers that project their point of views. The answers are broken down into four variables. They are named as "challenge1", "challenge2", and so on, to "challenge4" (table 11).

Twenty-one choices of respondents (37%) agree that the budget for PR is tight or little (challenge 4) is among challenges from their working environment. Eighteen choices (32%) state that the BOD has not had enough understandings about PR (challenge 2) is what PR practitioners are facing up in their work. Fifteen choices (26%) agree that one of their obstacles in PR works is the BOD do not spend enough money for PR activities (challenge 3). Three choices from respondents (5%) indicate that the board of directors did not trust expertise of PR team (challenge 1) is one of practitioners' challenges in their work.

4. How do you think you could solve these challenges (question 3) and how you evaluate its effectiveness?

For this question, the respondents could select multiple answers. The answers include three variables. They are "solution1", "solution2" and "solution3" (table 12). Furthermore, respondents are also requested to give their evaluation score of effectiveness to each of solution they chose (table 13). The table 12 and 13 show that sharing information, articles, studies about the role of PR to board of director (solution 1) is chosen by fifteen times (42%) from practitioners. Its evaluation score of effectiveness is 3.18 which fell to the "neutral" category.

Thirteen of selection from practitioners (36%) states that inviting BOD to join in PR seminars, symposium (solution 2) is one of the ways they can use to solve out the issue. The evaluation score of effectiveness of solution 2 is 3.2 which fell also to the "neutral" category. Eight of respondent's feedback (22%) indicates that resigning or quitting the company (solution 3) as the option to deal with challenges from working environment. The evaluation score of effectiveness of this solution is 2.68 which fell between the "disagree" and "neutral" category.

Part 2: For Agency PR practitioners

5. What are your own challenges you are facing up with in your works?

Clients steal the ideas (challenge 1) and PR team is not professional and high profile (challenge 4) are both chosen twenty-eight times by agency PR practitioners (27%) as their own challenges in works. Twenty-five of choices from them (24%) agree that clients make pressure for lower quotation (challenge 2) is one of their difficulties in works. Twenty-two of their selection (21%)

indicates that being invited for bidding as clients' bidding procedures (they need us to have enough 3 vendors' quotation) (challenge 3) is also the matter they need to solve out. Besides, agency PR practitioners have also highlighted other challenges from their own situation, such as they have not caught up the new PR movement and not been strong at negotiation with clients.

> *6. How do you think you could solve these challenges (question 5) and how you evaluate its effectiveness?*

For this question, the respondents are allowed to select multiple answers. The answer includes three variables. They are "solution1", "solution2", and "solution3" (table 15). In addition, respondents are also allowed to give their evaluation score of effectiveness to each of solution they selected (table 16).

Eighteen of choices from agency practitioners (34%) state that refuse the clients' request (because you see negative signals from clients) (solution 1) is their option to deal with the issue of steal the ideas. Seventeen of their selection (33%) answer that must-accept clients' requests (although recognizing negative signals from clients) (solution 2) and training for lower profile team member (solution 3) are ideas that are expected to improve their current issues.

The solution 1's evaluation score of effectiveness is 2.86 which fell between the "disagree" and "neutral" category. Similar to solution 1, that of solution 2 which is 2.75 fells between the "disagree" and "neutral" category as well, while that of solution 3 which is 3.73 fells near to the "agree" category. Besides, agency PR practitioners also suggest other solutions, such as sub-contracting to third parties, discussing internally on each client' request to choose suitable response and self-improving experiences to deal with these matters.

Part 3: For all PR practitioners

> *7. What do you expect to gain from the PR professional organisation?*

For this question, respondents could choose multiple answers. There are three answers which are also three variables. They are "expectation1", "expectation2" and "expectation3" (table 17).

Forty-five of selections from respondents (42%) state that opportunity to widen personal network with PR practitioners (expectation 1) is their concern expectation. Thirty-four of choices from them (32%) reply that celebrating in deep PR training courses (expectation 2) is one of their requirements from PR professional organisation, while twenty-eight of practitioners' choices (26%) answer that celebrating PR seminars/symposium for CEO, enterprises (expectation 3) to help them understand about PR is an initiative they need. Furthermore, practitioners have also suggested that PR practitioners should also gather to create an alliance to fight against clients' stealing their ideas and clients' making pressure on their quotation proposal.

> *8. What topics you are interested in PR seminars or training courses?*

For question 8, the respondents could choose multiple answers for PR topics they are interested in. The answers include five variables. They are "topic1", "topic2" and so on to "topic5 (table 18).

Forty of selections from respondents (26%) reply that crisis communication (topic 1) is one of their choices. Topic 2 "How to plan a PR strategy" is selected by thirty-eight of selections (25%). Twenty-seven (18%) indicate that internal communication (topic 3) is one of topic they want. Twenty-four (16%) answer that soft skill in PR (project management, presentation, writing skill…) (topic 5) is their chosen topic. Twenty-five (16%) state that bidding techniques of PR project (topic 4) is their choice.

9. *In your views, what could the PR professional organisation contribute to the PR industry in Vietnam?*

For this question, the respondents could choose multiple answers. The answers include two variables. They are "contribution1" and "contribution2" (table 19). Forty-seven of selections (70%) state that setting standards of professional practices to protect clients' right and agency's ideas (contribution 1) is one of contributions of PR professional organization to the PR industry of Vietnam. Twenty of choices (30%) answer that contribution 2 "celebrating award to honor PR campaigns of individual, organization that brings benefit to society" is the way the PR organization could contribute to PR industry.

10. *Do you agree to be member of the PR professional organisation?*

For this question, respondents could only choose one answer, yes or no (table 20). Fifty-two respondents (98%) agree to become member of the PR professional organisation while one person (2%) disagrees without any explanation.

11. *What do you think you could contribute to the PR professional organisation?*

For question 11, PR practitioners could choose multiple answers they are interested in. The answers include three variables. They are "contribution1", "contribution1" and "contribution3" (table 21).

Thirty-six of selections from respondents (41%) answer that participate in implementing activities of the organization (contribution 3) is the way of contribution. Thirty-five of selections (40%) reply that providing good ideas or initiatives for the organization activities (contribution 1) is one of their ideas of contribution. Seventeen of selections (19%) indicate that volunteer to join into core member of the organization (contribution 2) is the way they commit to contribute to PR organization. Besides, PR practitioners propose that they could contribute to PR professional organization by sharing their work experiences to other members and becoming bridge to connect people and encourage people to join in this organization.

> *12. How do you agree on the annual membership fee around 15 USD/person? And 13. How do you agree on the ticket fee of PR seminar/symposium around 10 USD/person?*

For this question, respondents reveal their level of agreement on suggested fees by rating-scale option (table 22). The mean score for annual membership fee (15 USD/person) is 3.48 and that of ticket fee of PR seminar/symposium is 3.49. They both fell between the "neutral" and "agree" category.

Findings and Discussion

In this section, the researcher discusses on what he found in the study. This study attempts to answer five research questions to reveal and project an updated picture of public relations situation and the need to form a professional organisation in Vietnam. Each question will be discussed one by one.

> *RQ 1 & RQ 2. What challenges PR practitioners in Vietnam are facing within their works? How do they think to solve these challenges themselves?*

For in-house PR practitioners:

Result from the study showed that there are eight challenges in works *come from themselves.* They are: lack of helpful relations (with Journalist, vendor, expert, influencer, opinion leader) (25%), lack of experience (17%), lack of specialized skills (11%), lack of PR knowledge (11%), lack of knowledge about the product / service / industry / business sector (14%), lack of study and research materials (10%), limitation of English communication (5%), limitation of employment information (2%).

The data of quantitative research answers that in-house practitioners are lack of helpful relations (25%). This result could be explained by findings of Hang Dinh (2010). In her study, Hang Dinh (2010) concluded that most of practitioners would take the execution role rather than the strategic planning role. Most of them are at executive level. They have not had enough privilege to access full relations with target audiences to run their works, such as business partners, authorities, vendors, shareholders, influencers, etc. So, practitioners naturally feel they are lack of relations for their works.

Besides, lack of experience (17%) and lack of specialized skills (11%) are also big challenges in works of in-house practitioners. It is understandable because PR began in Vietnam since 1990s and its practice is in its early dawn (Hang Dinh, 2010). Furthermore, in-house PR practitioners said that they are lack of study & research materials (10%). In fact, PR books and PR journals written by Vietnamese authors are very limited. The researcher himself has faced up many difficulties in doing Literature review of this study.

Practitioners have been lack of PR knowledge (11%) as well. To find explanation for this point, the researcher has conducted a searching study in the internet about number of universities and training centers that are teaching PR in Vietnam. The result (appendix F) showed that there are only two universities lecturing post-graduate level, six universities teaching bachelor level and five training centers teaching certificate level of PR in Vietnam.

The data of online survey indicated that in-house practitioners are being lack of knowledge about the product / service / industry / business sector (14%). This result of online survey contradicts with that of in-dept interview. While the result of quantitative research ranged lack of knowledge as one of the third biggest challenges of practitioners, the result of qualitative research said that it is not reasonable. On the contrary, one practitioner highlighted, during an interview, that:

> *Before being assigned any communication tasks, in-house practitioner must have been trained clearly about the organization he/she is working for, such corporate background, brands, products/service, industry, competitors, etc. In my opinion, all companies will have trained their PR staff. So he/she could not say that lack of knowledge about these things is his/her challenge in works (Personal communication, January, 5, 2015)*

To explain for the conflict of this argument, the researcher thinks because there may not all organizations which implemented full and deep training course for their PR staff as well as practitioners are often advised to do self-studying, so practitioners will naturally feel lack of knowledge on products/service, industry, competitors, etc. In reality, even they self-study hard, they could not earn enough knowledge about law related to their products/services as well as their competitors' activities through years.

The survey found that limitation of English communication is the least concerns of practitioners. Most of PR practitioners are confident with their English proficiency. However, this result goes completely contrary to the initial assessment of the researcher, because foreign language proficiency is considered as a greatest barrier and "nightmare" of Vietnamese young workers now (Vietnam News Government Press, 2014). To explain for this result, one PR practitioner shared the truth:

> *English proficiency is very important to any PR practitioner. So, in the beginning of recruitment process, we conduct English test to choose good English-using candidates to invite them to go on interview round (Personal communication, January, 7, 2015).*

This explanation could be used to explain why minority of respondents who are current PR practitioners agree that limit of English expertise is not really their challenge. They must be firstly a good English communicator, then to become the current PR practitioner of a certain organization. Finally, the minority of practitioners agree that limitation of employment information (2%) is their problem although there is no PR association or PR practitioner network in Vietnam. The researcher has not collected successfully any satisfactory explanation for this result yet.

To solve out challenges come from themselves, in-house practitioners has selected five solutions, such as "establishing new relationship through current connections" (30%, 3.81), "participating in seminars, networking events" (25%, 3.53), "searching further information in local and international magazine, newspaper and internet" (25%, 3.53), "participating in related training courses" (20%, 3.56) and "searching career opportunities from head hunters, internet" (1%, 2.46).

It is notable that most of average score of effectiveness of solutions fluctuates between 3 "neutral" to 4 "agree". There is no solution which is scored at 3 or at 4. This finding showed that practitioners are not totally confident at any solution. However, they tend to agree to choose solution which is suggested to solve out their challenges. They have had no added solutions.

Result from the study also emphasized that there are four challenges in works *come from their working environment.* They are: the budget for PR is tight or little (37%), their BOD has not had enough understandings about PR (32%), their BOD do not allocate enough money for PR activities (26%), their BOD did not trust expertise of PR team (5%).

Most people do not fully understand about public relations (Vietnamnews, 2014) and PR practice in Vietnam is in its early stage (Hang Dinh, 2010) could be main reasons to explain for why BOD have not supported PR activities. They may have limited understandings about PR. Besides, practitioners may have not implemented PR activities successfully, so they could not win BOD's trust and earn for better budget allocation.

To solve out challenges come from working environment, in-house practitioners has selected three solutions. They are "sharing information, articles, studies about the role of PR to board of director" (42%, 3.18), "inviting BOD to join in PR seminars, symposium (36%, 3.2)" and "resigning or quitting the company" (22%, 2.68).

Different to the score of effectiveness of solutions for challenges coming from themselves, that of solutions for challenges coming from working environment fluctuates between 2 "disagree" to 3 "neutral". This finding showed that practitioners are neither completely confident in effectiveness nor agree with solutions they chose. Besides three solution suggested by questionnaire, practitioners have no added suggestion. The answer and thinking about this challenge may not be ready in their mind though it is their obstacles in work.

For agency PR practitioners:

Result from the study showed that agency PR practitioners have faced up four challenges in their works, such as "clients steal their ideas" (27%), "clients make pressure for lower quotation"

(24%), "being invited for bidding as clients' bidding procedures" (21%) and "PR team is not professional & high profile" (27%).

The first three results of the study ("clients steal the ideas", "clients make pressure for lower quotation" (24%), "being invited for bidding as clients' bidding procedures") have emphasized again observation of Le Thu Quyen (Vietnamnews, 2014) that many PR agencies have focused on lowering prices to win contracts instead of improving their service quality. This may create a bad habit in clients to searching for agencies who accept for lower quotation. If agencies do not accept, they will remove their name out of the vendor list and cooperate with another one. In addition, there is no current specific law or PR standardization to protect agencies' intellectual property rights (Hang Dinh, 2010; Vietnamnews 2014), so it is easy to understand that why agencies' ideas has been stolen.

One agency practitioner noted that:

> *In this aggressive competition among PR agencies, client is king. They are kings because they could go shopping for your ideas without any payment. They just need to ask you submit your proposal and they got what they want. You could not provide them a bad idea because it represents your image. That's the vicious cycle. (Personal communication, January, 3, 2015)*

Another practitioner shares the same ideas that:

> *Even I know that there is nothing I could gain from the proposal we are asked to submit by clients, I must do it. I do it with the very painful feeling because my ideas and my efforts are wasteful. They need my proposal to earn for three options. It is good for their buying procurement. (Personal communication, January, 4, 2015)*

The results "PR team is not professional & high profile" has similar to observation of Nguyen Thanh Dao (Vietnamnews, 2014) that PR industry in Vietnam is the lack of good PR professionals. For these challenges above, agency PR practitioners has selected three solutions to solve out three challenges accordingly. They decide to refuse the clients' request (because they see negative signals from clients) (34%, 2.86). They must accept clients' requests (although recognizing negative signals from clients) (33%, 2.75), and train for lower profile team member (33%, 3.73).

The results have provided an interesting finding that although agency PR practitioners know how to respond to their clients' negative request (refuse or accept), they do not agree on these solutions they chose. The score of effectiveness of these solutions is between 2 "disagree" and 3 "neutral". They added that they should deal with clients' request case-by-case and sub-contract to the third parties to avoid risks and ineffectiveness. Additionally, on how to deal with challenge of PR team low expertise, most of practitioners agree the solution of training for their teammate in projects and they are fairly confident on this tasks.

RQ 3. How do they think a PR professional organisation can support to solve their problems?

Result in the study showed that all PR practitioners agree the PR professional organization could help them to solve their challenges. They expect this organization could support them to widen their network and open connections with other practitioners (42%), provide them useful training course (32%) and celebrate PR seminar to help their BOD understand about PR role (26%).

Besides, agency practitioners expect this PR professional organization to become a force to fight against clients' negative requests. They believe that it is the perfect solution. One reputable practitioner, in an interview, suggested that:

> *Agency PR practitioners should gather to set a benchmark of fees, including idea fee, proposal fee, consulting fee per hour to protect our intellectual property. All agencies must do together so that our challenges could be solved out. But I noted that although this idea began five year ago, it has not come true because we have not been able to be gathered. Agencies seem too busy with satisfying their clients (Personal communication, December, 15, 2014)*

An established scholar PR practitioner explained that:

> *There have been several meetings to discuss on establishing the PR association to ensure healthy career development and ethics compliance. I am myself as an active member to run this project. However, there is not many PR agency have commitment of contribution of time and financial resources. (Personal communication, December, 15, 2014)*

An MD of famous PR firms shared that:

> *We are in the same page that we need the PR association. However, we have different ideas on how it works. I think that PR association must firstly bring benefits to PR agency, then to in-house practitioners. Remember that in-house practitioner is the client of PR agency practitioners. We have conflicted benefits which could not be harmonized well. That is reason why establishing PR association is difficult. (Personal communication, December, 15, 2014)*

The fourth PR practitioner who has15 years of experiences shared her point:

> *In-house and agency PR practitioner need PR association. Even PR freelancers need PR association to protect them. We all need the PR association. But we could not have one this time, because we have no excellent proponent to call for establishing PR association. He or she must be a person who has both big successes in his business and high academic qualifications in PR field that are admired by many practitioners. We have no man like that this time. We could not follow one who we did not accept as our leader. (Personal communication, December, 15, 2014)*

In this case, to overcome all above issues, all interviewees agree that government should be the advocacy to established PR association in Vietnam. The PR association should be the non-profit company which headed by the government.

Last but not least, practitioners expect that PR professional organization could also provide them useful training course (32%). The quantitative data showed that most of practitioners selected "crisis communication", "how to plan a PR strategy" and "internal communication" are their most interested training topics. This may indicate that the need to do more advanced work of Vietnamese practitioners is being increased.

> *RQ 4. How do they think a PR professional organisation can also contribute to the development of PR industry in Vietnam, especially when AEC is established?*

Most of PR practitioners think PR association could contribute to the PR industry by: setting standards of professional practices to protect clients' right and agency's ideas (70%) and celebrating award to honor PR campaigns of individual, organization that brings benefit to society (30%). PR practitioners added their opinion on this point which researcher totally agrees:

> *PR association should be the bridge between PR practitioners,* business organisations *and the government. Business organisations' voice and PR practitioners' voice could be transferred to government through PR association and vice versa. It makes the PR industry as well as the business environment healthier and stronger especially when AEC is established. PR association should also become a trusted unit to help business enterprises in promoting brands within ASEAN and the world. (Personal communication, December, 15, 2014)*

> *RQ 5. How do they think they can contribute to this PR professional organisation?*

Result in the study showed that PR practitioners think they could contribute for the PR professional organisation by: participating in implementing activities of the organization (41%), providing good ideas or initiatives for the organization activities (40%), volunteer to join into core member of the organization (19%). Besides, they would want to share their experiences to others and encourage people to join in this organization.

Thus, it is easy to understand why 98% practitioners agree to become member of PR association. The rest 2% disagree to join in because they are very busy at work and could not commit on their time. In addition, the annual membership fee (15 USD) and ticket fee (10 USD) for every PR seminar may be high for most of practitioners. However, the researcher believes that it is not matter of how much the fee is. The fee should be set at the value of benefits that the PR association could bring to its members.

The next section "Conclusion" will present the limitations and suggestions for future study as well as the implications for practitioners.

CHAPTER 5

CONCLUSION

Limitations and suggestions for future study

The study aims to contribute toward the scope of the foundation of PR association in Vietnam which has not ever been touched before. It looks into the challenges, needs and expectations within the PR practitioner community in Vietnam. Though the study could reveal important hidden corners of the PR industry in Vietnam, it has some limitations.

The first limitation of this study is its small sample size. The total respondents of this research are 53 people. It is too small to generalize for all of practitioners in Vietnam. For this reason, future studies should find more practitioners to do a nationwide study. Doing that way could generalize better findings.

The second limitation of this study lies in its methodology. The methodology has been used are online survey and in-dept interview. Though the researchers has gained important analysis information about the PR industry, but he did not actually get points of view from law makers, business men and general public about this industry. For this reason, the researcher assumes that a study that employed law makers, business men and citizen might yield better results.

According to the researcher, there are many topics that should be researched to have more comprehensive picture about PR industry in Vietnam. They might be (a) What law makers think about PR association, what its role and how it could contribute to state management about information and commercial competition and (b) What business men think about PR contribution to their business goal: advantages and disadvantages. Those two topics above continue this study toward greater extent. In viewpoint of researcher, they are very practical and important to PR industry in Vietnam.

The next limitation is the Findings chapter may be so long. It is long because the author desires to find out clearly what challenges PR professionals are facing with, how they think they could solve these issues themselves and what they expect on the PR association in helping them to solve these challenges. Although the author believes the length of the Finding chapter may be long to reflect successfully the general picture of PR industry in Vietnam, it is satisfied with standard of an academic dissertation.

The fourth limitation of this study is its limited academic references for literature review. In Vietnam, PR is in its new dawn. The source of PR academic research is very few. So, discussion chapter just have nearly enough referencing to literature review. Moreover, this research topic about the PR industry in Vietnam is the very first one. There are many challenges for the author in doing this research, such as there are limited PR academic materials in Vietnam, there are limited reputable PR professionals who are ready to share their thinking and there are limited time and budget for this research. So, the author has tried his best much more than ever to complete this research, instead of choosing easier topics. The author hopes that though this dissertation needs far more improvement, it could help much for Vietnamese communication students who would want to study about PR industry of Vietnam.

Implications for practitioners

First, the study results suggest that PR association in Vietnam should be established and that government should be the advocacy to establish it. The PR association should be the non-profit company which headed by the government. If there were a PR association in Vietnam, PR practitioners and business organisations would gain much benefit from it. PR practitioners would have their "home" to open their network and career development opportunities, while business organisations could achieve their business goals through effective and ethic PR practices. Moreover, they could have a PR association to claim for and solve out dirty communication activities of their competitors.

Second, the study results suggest that practitioners should be more active to gather to run for PR association establishment. Being a PR practitioner, the researcher understands that practitioners are very busy with their daily works. However, if we have more finance or/and time contribution from practitioners, we could make it successfully.

Findings and Results

RQ 1 & RQ 2. What challenges PR practitioners in Vietnam are facing within their works? How do they think to solve these challenges themselves?

For in-house PR practitioners:

The study results showed that, coming from in-house practitioners themselves, there are eight challenges in their works, such as: "lack of helpful relations (with Journalist, vendor, expert, influencer, opinion leader)"; "lack of experience"; "lack of specialized skills"; "lack of PR knowledge"; "lack of knowledge about the product/service /industry/business sector"; "lack of study and research materials"; "limitation of English communication"; and "limitation of employment information".

To solve out challenges themselves, in-house practitioners has five solutions to improving their expertise and career development opportunities themselves, such as: "establishing new relationship through current connections"; "participating in seminars, networking events"; "searching further information in local and international magazine, newspaper and internet";

"participating in related training courses"; and "searching career opportunities from head hunters, internet".

The study results also showed that, coming from working environment, there are four challenges in works that practitioners are facing up. They are "the budget for PR is tight"; "their BOD has not had enough understandings about PR"; "their BOD do not allocate enough money for PR activities" and "their BOD did not trust expertise of PR team".

To solve out those four challenges, in-house practitioners has three solutions. Two of them aim to help their boss understand about PR, such as "sharing information, articles, studies about the role of PR to board of director" and "inviting BOD to join in PR seminars, symposium". If these two solutions do not work, they choose the last solution "resigning or quitting the company".

It is important to notice that practitioners are neither completely confident in effectiveness nor agree with solutions they chose. Besides three solution suggested by questionnaire, practitioners have no added suggestions. The answer and thinking about this challenge may not be ready in their mind though it is their obstacles in work.

For agency PR practitioners:

Result from the study showed that agency PR practitioners have faced up four challenges in their works, such as "clients steal their ideas", "clients make pressure for lower quotation", "being invited for bidding as clients' bidding procedures" and "PR team is not professional & high profile".

To overcome these challenges, agency PR practitioners has selected three responses. They "refuse the clients' request because they see negative signals from clients", or in many case they "must accept clients' requests although recognizing negative signals from clients", and "do training for lower profile team member".

The results have provided an interesting finding that although agency PR practitioners know how to respond to their clients' negative request (refuse or accept), they do not agree on these solutions they chose. They added that they should deal with clients' request case-by-case and sub-contract to the third parties to avoid risks and ineffectiveness. Additionally, on how to deal with challenge of PR team low expertise, most of practitioners agree the solution of doing training for their teammate in projects and they are fairly confident on this tasks.

RQ 3. How do they think a PR professional organisation can support to solve their problems?

The study results showed that all PR practitioners agree that the PR professional organisation (or PR association) could help them to solve their challenges. They think that this organization could support them to "widen their network and open connections with other practitioners", "provide them useful training course" and "celebrate PR seminar to help their BOD understand about PR role".

Besides, agency practitioners expect this PR professional organization to become a force to fight against clients' negative requests because it set up code of conduct for the whole PR industry, and the benchmark of fees, including idea fee, proposal fee, consulting fee to protect practitioners' intellectual property.

However, it is not easy to establish the PR association in Vietnam. They explain that there is still not PR association in Vietnam because practitioners have not been able to be gathered due to lack of the qualified advocacy/proponent, benefit conflict and no commitment of contribution of time and financial resources. They agree that government should be the advocacy to establish PR association to overcome these issues.

RQ 4. How do they think a PR professional organisation can also contribute to the development of PR industry in Vietnam, especially when AEC is established?

The study results projected that the PR professional organisation could contribute to the PR industry by "setting standards of professional practices to protect clients' right and agency's ideas" and "celebrating award to honor PR campaigns of individual, organization that brings benefit to society". Moreover, the PR professional organisation (or PR association) should be the bridge among PR practitioners, business organisations and the government. Business organisations' voice and PR practitioners' voice could be transferred to government through PR association and vice versa. It makes the PR industry and the business environment healthier and stronger especially when AEC is established. PR association should also be the trusted unit to help business enterprises in promoting brands within ASEAN and the world.

RQ 5. How do PR practitioners think they can contribute to this PR professional organisation?

The study results showed that most of PR practitioners think they could contribute for the PR professional organisation by "participating in implementing activities of the organization"; "providing good ideas or initiatives for the organization activities"; "volunteer to join into core member of the organization". Besides, they would want to share their experiences to others and encourage people to join in this organization.

In addition, the annual membership fee (15 USD) and ticket fee (10 USD) for each PR seminar may be high for them. However, the researcher believes that it is not matter of how much the fee is. The fee should be set at the value of benefits that the PR association could bring to its members.

Conclusion

PR industry in Vietnam is in its early dawn so it might take long time to have the PR association. However, the researcher hopes that this study could contribute a helpful voice to alert about the need of a PR professional organisation (or PR association) in Vietnam. It is hoped that Vietnam will be able to shape its way to give birth of an excellent and professional PR organisation in future./.

APPENDICES

COVER LETTER FOR INTERVIEW PARTICIPANTS

Re: Invite for research interview

Dear: ---

My name is Le Tran Bao Phuong. I am the graduate student of the University ofStirling (UK).

To collect data for the research **"Public Relations and the need to form a professional organisation in Vietnam",** I use the interview method and online survey. I am hoping you would be willing to participate for the interview because you opinions would be invaluable and meaningful to us as well as PR operations in Vietnam.

The research findings will help people understand more deeply about the challenges and obstacles that PR practitioners are facing up with in their works as well as the positive solutions, the level of urgency to establish a professional organisation of public relations in Vietnam and the expected value from this organisation's activities.

This interview section will take about 30 minutes to complete. The interview questions is only related to your viewpoints, and is not related to any private information.

Your participation in the survey is voluntary without reward. However, you will receive my summary of research findings upon completion. Your answer will be kept confidential. Thank you very much and I look forward to cooperate with you,

Le Tran Bao Phuong

APPENDIX B

IN-DEPTH INTERVIEW QUESTIONS

1. **Personal Information**

- Full name:
- Gender:

- Organisation:
- Position:
- Location:
- Year of experiences:
- Major of study:

2. Challenges of PR practitioners in Vietnam

2.1. In your opinion, how to understand correctly about public relations? What is the main role of PR practitioner in a business enterprise?

*For PR practitioners from **in-house***

2.2. In your view, what are challenges these PR practitioners from in-house are facing up with in their works, from their own situation and from the working environment?

2.3. Could you please advise them how they solve their own challenges themselves?

*For PR practitioners from **agency***

2.4. In your view, what are challenges these PR practitioners from agency in their works, from their own situation and from the working environment?

2.5. Could you please advise them how they solve their own challenges themselves?

3. The need of a PR professional organisation

3.1 Do you think Vietnam should have a PR professional organisation? And why?

3.2 In your view, why there is still no PR professional organisation in Vietnam until now?

3.3 What do you expect to gain from the PR professional organisation?

3.4 In your views, what could the PR professional organisation contribute to the PR industry in Vietnam?

3.5 What do you think you could contribute to the PR professional organisation?

COVERING LETTER TO SURVEY PARTICIPANTS

Re: Invite for participation of online survey

Dear: --

My name is Le Tran Bao Phuong. I am the graduate student of the University ofStirling (UK).

To collect data for the research **"Public Relations and the need to form a professional organisation in Vietnam",** I use the online survey and interview method. I hope that you will assist me by completing the survey because you opinions would be invaluable and meaningful to us as well as PR operations in Vietnam.

The research findings will help people understand more deeply about the challenges and obstacles that PR practitioners are facing up with in their works as well as the positive solutions, the level of urgency to establish a professional organisation of public relations in Vietnam and the expected value from this organisation's activities.

This questionnaire will take 15 minutes to complete. The survey content is only related to your viewpoints, and is not related to any private information.

Your participation in the survey is voluntary without reward. However, you will receive my summary of research findings upon completion. Your answer will be kept confidential. Thank you very much and I look forward to cooperate with you,

Le Tran Bao Phuong

APPENDIX D

QUESTIONNAIRES

PUBLIC RELATIONS AND THE NEED TO FORM A PROFESSIONAL ORGANISATION IN VIETNAM

This questionnaire will take you 15 minutes to complete. If you have any questions or suggestions, please contact me at the email address letranbaophuong.2301@gmail.com. Your participation in the survey is voluntary. You can stop at any time. Your answer will be kept confidential.

Thank you very much.

PART I: For those who did work or has been working at **PR IN-HOUSE.**

Please kindly share your opinions on questions 1 – 4:

1. What are <u>your own challenges</u> you are facing up with in your works? (you can select 1 or more answers)

- ☐ Lack of helpful relations (with Journalist, vendor, expert, influencer, opinion leader)
- ☐ Lack of PR knowledge
- ☐ Lack of specialized skills (writing, planning, managing risks and crisis, establishing relationship…)
- ☐ Lack of knowledge about the product / service / industry / business sector
- ☐ Lack of experience
- ☐ Lack of study, research materials
- ☐ Limitation of English communication
- ☐ Limitation of employment information
- ☐ Other (please specify):

----

2. How do you think you could solve your own challenges yourself (question 1) and how you evaluate its effectiveness?

	Very ineffective	Ineffective	Neutral	Effective	Very Effective
☐ Establish new relationship through current connections	○	○	○	○	○
☐ Participate in seminars, networking events	○	○	○	○	○
☐ Participate in related training courses	○	○	○	○	○
☐ Search further information in local and international magazine and newspaper, internet	○	○	○	○	○
☐ Search career opportunities from head	○	○	○	○	○

| hunters, internet
☐ Other:
....
.... | ○   ○   ○   ○   ○ |

3. What are challenges <u>from working environment</u> you are facing up with in your works?
(you can select 1 or more answers)

    ☐ The board of directors (BOD) do not trust expertise of PR team
    ☐ The BOD has not had enough understandings about PR
    ☐ The BOD do not spend enough for PR activities
    ☐ The budget for PR is tight or little
    ☐ Other challenges from BOD:

----

4. How do you think you could solve these challenges (question 3) and how you evaluate its effectiveness?

	Very ineffective	Ineffective	Neutral	Effective	Very Effective
☐ Sharing information, articles, studies about the role of PR to BOD	○	○	○	○	○
☐ Invite BOD to join in PR seminars, symposium	○	○	○	○	○
☐ Resign or quit the company	○	○	○	○	○
☐ Other:	○	○	○	○	○

PART 2: For those who did work or has been working at PR AGENCY.

Please kindly share your opinions on questions 5 - 6:

5. What are <u>your own challenges</u> you are facing up with in your works? (you can select 1 or more answers)

    ☐ Clients steal the ideas
    ☐ Clients make pressure for lower quotation
    ☐ Be invited for bidding as clients' bidding procedures (they need 3 vendors' quotation)
    ☐ PR team is not professional and high profile

☐   Other:

----

6. How do you think you could solve these challenges (question 5) and how you evaluate its effectiveness?

	Very ineffective	Ineffective	Neutral	Effective	Very Effective
☐ Refuse the clients' request (because you see negative signals from clients)	○	○	○	○	○
☐ Accept (although you see negative signals from clients)	○	○	○	○	○
☐ Training for lower profile team member	○	○	○	○	○
☐ Other:	○	○	○	○	○
....					
....					

PART 3: For all PR practitioners

7. What do you expect to gain from the PR professional organisation?

☐   Opportunity to widen personal network with PR practitioners
☐   Celebrate in deep PR training courses
☐   Celebrate PR seminars/symposium for CEO, enterprises
☐   Other:

----

8. What topics you are interested in PR seminars or training courses? (you could choose 1 or more answers)

☐   Crisis communication
☐   How to plan a PR strategy
☐   Internal communication
☐   Bidding techniques of PR project
☐   Soft skill in PR (project management, presentation, writing skill...)
☐   Other:

----

9. In your views, what could the PR professional organisation contribute to the PR industry in Vietnam? (you could choose 1 or more answers)

☐ Set standards of professional practices to protect clients' right and agency's ideas)
☐ Celebrate award to honor PR campaigns of individual, organisation that brings benefit to society.
☐ Other:

----

10. Do you agree to be member of the PR professional organisation?

☐   Yes
☐   No

11. What do you think you could contribute to the PR professional organisation?

☐ Good ideas or initiatives for this organisation activities
☐ Volunteer to join into core member of the organisation
☐ Participate in implementing activities of the organisation
☐ Other contribution:

----

12. How do you agree on the annual membership fee as 300,000 VNĐ/person?

Very disagree ....Totally agree
       1   2   3   4   5

13. How do you agree on the ticket fee of PR seminar/symposium as 200,000 VND/person?

Very disagree ....Totally agree
       1   2   3   4   5

PART 4

This part consist questions about your personal information. Your information is kept confidential. The purpose of part II is to differentiate respondents.

1. Full name: ---
2. Age: ---
3. Sex:
   - ☐ Female
   - ☐ Male
4. Where are you working now?
   - ☐ Ho Chi Minh
   - ☐ Ha Noi
   - ☐ Other place:--
5. How long have you been working in PR field?
   - ☐ < 1 year
   - ☐ From 1 – 3 year
   - ☐ From 3 – 5 year
   - ☐ From 5 – 10 year
   - ☐ > 10 year
6. Are you in management position in PR now?
   - ☐ Yes
   - ☐ No

Many thanks for your participation in the survey!

DATA TABLES

Table 1: Gender of respondent

		Count	Percent
Sex	Male	22	42
	Female	31	58

Table 2: Location of respondents

		Count	Percent
City	HCM City	44	83
	Ha Noi	4	7.5
	Other	5	9.5

Table 3: Breakdown of respondents by Age and Sex

		Sex	
		Male	Female
		Count	Count
Age	18-22	1	0
	23-30	16	19
	30-40	5	10
	40-60	0	2
	>60	0	0

Table 4: Working experience of respondents

		Count
Working Experience	<1 year	4
	1-3 years	24
	3-5 years	14
	5-10 years	8
	>10 years	3

	Working Experience				
	<1 year	1-3 years	3-5 years	5-10 years	>10 years
	Count	Count	Count	Count	Count

Managerial postion	Yes	0	7	9	7	3
	No	4	17	5	1	0

Table 5: Breakdown of respondents by Work experience and Managerial position

Age * Managerial Position Crosstabulation				
Count				
		Managerial Position		
		Yes	No	Total
Age	18-22	0	1	1
	23-30	11	24	35
	30-40	13	2	15
	40-60	2	0	2
Total		26	27	53

Table 6: Breakdown of respondents by Managerial position and Sex

		Sex	
		Male	Female
		Count	Count
Managerial position	Yes	13	13
	No	9	18

Table 7: Breakdown of respondents by Managerial position and Age

		Age									
		18-22		23-30		30-40		40-60		>60	
		Sex		Sex		Sex		Sex		Sex	
		Male	Female	Male	Female	Male	Female	Male	Female	Male	Female
		Count	Count	Count	Count	Count	Count	Count	Count	Count	Count
Managerial position	Yes	0	0	8	3	5	8	0	2	0	0
	No	1	0	7	16	0	2	0	0	0	0

Table 8: Challenges of own in-house PR practitioners in their works

	Challenge 1	Challenge 2	Challenge 3	Challenge 4	Challenge 5	Challenge 6	Challenge 7	Challenge 8
Count	21	11	11	12	14	8	4	2
Percent	25%	13%	13%	14%	17%	10%	5%	2%

Table 9: Solution of in-house PR practitioners for their own challenges

	Solution 1	Solution 2	Solution 3	Solution 4	Solution 5
Count	24	20	16	20	1
Percent	30%	25%	20%	25%	1%

Table 10: The average evaluation score of effectiveness of each solution for their own challenges

	Solution 1	Solution 2	Solution 3	Solution 4	Solution 5
Average rate	3.81	3.53	3.56	3.59	2.46

Table 11: Challenges of in-house PR practitioners in their works from working environment

	Challenge 1	Challenge 2	Challenge 3	Challenge 4
Count	3	18	15	21
Percent	5%	32%	26%	37%

Table 12: Solution of in-house PR practitioners for challenges from working environment

	Solution 1	Solution 2	Solution 3
Count	15	13	8
Percent	42%	36%	22%

Table 13: The average evaluation score of effectiveness of each solution for challenges from working environment

	Solution 1	Solution 2	Solution 3
Average rate	3.18	3.20	2.68

Table 14: Challenges of own agency PR practitioners in their works

	Challenge 1	Challenge 2	Challenge 3	Challenge 4
Count	28	25	22	28
Percent	27%	24%	21%	27%

Table 15: Solution of agency PR practitioners for their own challenges

	Solution 1	Solution 2	Solution 3
Count	18	17	17
Percent	34%	33%	33%

Table 16: The average evaluation score of effectiveness of each solution for agency practitioners' challenges

	Solution 1	Solution 2	Solution 3
Average rate	2.86	2.75	3.73

Table 17: Expectation of PR practitioners from PR professional organisation

	Expectation 1	Expectation 2	Expectation 3
Count	45	34	28
Percent	42%	32%	26%

Table 18: PR topics in which are interested by PR practitioners

	PR topic 1	PR topic 2	PR topic 3	PR topic 4	PR topic 5
Count	40	38	27	24	25
Percent	26%	25%	18%	16%	16%

Table 19: Contribution of PR professional organisation to the PR industry

	Contribution 1	Contribution 2
Count	47	20
Percent	70%	30%

Table 20: Agree to be member of the PR professional organisation

	Agree	Disagree
Count	52	1
Percent	98%	2%

Table 21: Contribution of PR practitioners to the PR professional organisation

	Contribution 1	Contribution 2	Contribution 3
Count	35	17	36
Percent	40%	19%	41%

Table 22: Agree on the annual membership fee of the PR association and the ticket fee of PR seminar/symposium

Agreement	Annual Fee	Seminar Fee
Average rate	3.48	3.49

APPENDIX F

UNIVERSITIES AND TRAINING CENTRES TEACHING PR IN VIET NAM

No		Name	Description	Location	Entity	Remark
Post graduate level						
1		University of Stirling (UK)	MSc degree in public relations is an interdisciplinary program and its emphasis is on professional administration rather than vocational training. This program aims to help students to develop a deeper understanding of the role of public relations in contemporary society and to develop skills such as analysis, management, communication and teamwork skills.	HCM	Foreign Univeristy	Full time: 1 year Part time: 2 years
2		Academy of Journalism and Communication	Founded in 2006, this faculty provided the first degree course of public relations and advertising in Vietnam. Its core aim is to train professionals working in communication field and to become a leading research center of public relations and advertising.	Ha Noi	Academy of Political and Administrative o f Ho Chi Minh City (under the Ministry of Internal Affairs)	Level of training: master and bachelor
University level						
3		Van Lang University	Training for university level of PR program, 4 years, enrollment began in 2007 with the implementation of block A, C, D.	HCM	Ministry of Education and Training	4 years

4	RMIT Vietnam	More than ever before, organisations are realising the need to communicate clearly with the public. This is harder than it sounds, and they need experts to help them with what to say, how and where to say it, and who to say it to. That's where professional communication graduates come in. It's not just about selling; it's about building relationships that will benefit both your company, and your community. This is essential to any organisation attempting to develop an effective integrated marketing communication mix.	HCM	Asia branch of RMIT HQ at Melbourne - Australia	4 years
5	Diplomatic Academy of Vietnam	Training for Bachelor of International Communication who have political qualities, professional behavior, health and ability to resolve the areas of expertise to meet the country's development requirements and international integration of Vietnam.	Ha Noi	Ministry of Foreign Affair	4 years
6	University of Technology HCM	The faculty provided specialized in training for students, equipping them with the knowledge, skills and operational methods of PR, which provide the basic knowledge and practical experience in PR. Armed with skills for learners to be able to organize events effectively with appropriate cost, and know how to prevent or minimize the risks arising in the process of organizing events. After graduation this, students can work in the editorial, television stations, advertising companies, corporate event companies at home and abroad.	HCM	Ministry of Education and Training	college

7	University of Social Sciences and Humanities	The Faculty of Journalism and Communication is one of the first university teaching PR in Vietnam (from 2001). Hundreds of alumni of the Faculty is responsible for the high position in the field of PR. With 50 targets for 2013 enrollment, for the first time, the Faculty of Journalism and Communication enroll the Bachelor of Public Relations.	Ha Noi	Vietnam National University (under the direct management of the Prime Minister)	
8	The Institute of Asian Studies	PUBLIC RELATIONS course of the Institute of Asian Studies (IAS) will give you the knowledge and experience trained by professional international level to implement these matters! After completing the course, you can perform your job more effectively through the grasp of knowledge about PR, as well as valuable experience of PR.	HCM	Ministry of Science & Technology	3 years
Certificate level					
9	LCCI Vietnam	LCCI stands for London Chamber of Commerce and Industry (London Association of Commerce and Industry), one of the most prestigious business qualifications in the world since 1887. International Qualifications of LCCI are provided by EDI , a leading service company for vocational and professional training in England.	HCM	branch of LCCI in Vietnam (LCCI presents in 125 countries)	3 months

				a member of Business Management Group - training center for International programs of England in Vietnam	
10	BMG International Education	After graduation, student are absolutely confident in planning for PR strategy, event management, press conferences and establishing relations with the group of public, media ...	HCM	a member of Business Management Group - training center for International programs of England in Vietnam	3 months
11	ARTI	Based on the philosophy of How to do, ARTI Vietnam has designed the training program to bring high practical content to help students Study for the best. With knowledge provides succinctly and concisely, along with the training of professional skills that can be applied immediately on the job every day, lectures will guide students thinking properly to achieve professional development in a professional efficiently.	HCM, Ha Noi	Vietnam Institute of Advertising	4 months
12	Management Quality Institute	During this time, exploiting the strengths of PR on sales activity is urgent, because the shopping season is evetful and inventory is over many times.	Da Nang, Binh Dinh, BRVT, Tay Ninh	Department of Science and Technology Ho Chi Minh City	2 days
13	HCMC Vocational College of Economics and Technology	The program focused on practice to address the situation of enterprise	HCM	Ministry of Labour - Invalids and Social Affairs	3 months

Bibliography

1. ASEAN. (2014). *ASEAN Economic Community.* At
   http://www.asean.org/communities/asean-economic-community [Accessed: 2 Jan 2015]
2. Black, P., Bastos, S., & Saxby, S. (2009). *Public relations in Vietnam: The social
   environment.* Retrieved from http://www.prinvietnam.net/social.html
3. Bong R. Osorio. (2014). *Working towards one ASEAN.* At
   http://www.philstar.com/business-life/2014/06/09/1332119/working-towards-one-asean
   [Access: 16 December 2014]
4. Bruce C. McKinney (2000). *Public Relations in the Land of Ascending Dragon:
   Implications in Light of the US/Vietnam Bilateral Trade Agreement.* Public Relations,
   Quarterly, 45 (4), 23-26.
5. Bruce C. McKinney (2006). *Public Relations in Vietnam: A Six-Year Perspective. Public
   Relations Quarterly,* 51 (2), 18-22.
6. Chen, N., & Culbertson, H. M. (1996a). Guest relations: A demanding but constrained
   role for lady public relations practitioners in mainland China. Public Relations Review,
   22, 279–296.
7. Chen, N., & Culbertson, H. M. (1996b November). Public relations education in the
   People's Republic of China: A tentative look at the process. Paper presented at the
   meeting the Association for the Advancement of Policy, Research, and Development in
   the Third World, Cancun, Mexico.
8. CIPR. (2014). *Definition of PR.* At http://www.cipr.co.uk/content/careers-cpd/careers-
   advice-and-case-studies/what-pr [Access: 20 December, 2014]
9. CIPR. (2014). *About us.* At http://www.cipr.co.uk/content/about-us/mission-vision-and-
   values [Accessed: 03 January 2015]
10. Curtin, P. A., & Gaither, T. K. (2007). *International public relations: Negotiating
    culture, identity, and power.* Sage Publications.
11. Daniel Lerner, *"Communications System and Social Systems: Statistical Exploration in
    History and Policy,"* Behavioral Science, No. 2, Oct. 1957, tr. 266-275. Daniel Lerner,
    "Systèmes de communications et systèmessociaux", in Francis Balleand Jean Padioleau
    (Ed.), Sociologie de l'information, Textesfondamentaux, Paris, Larousse, 1973, p. 142
12. Curtin P. A. & Gaither T. K., (2007). *International public relations. Negotiating culture,
    identity and power.* USA: Sage.
13. Vietnam Government Press News (VGP News). (2014). *Foreign language: the fear of
    the youth labour (Ngoại ngữ: "Nỗi sợ" của lao động trẻ).* Retrieved from:
    http://baodientu.chinhphu.vn/Doi-song/Ngoai-ngu-Noi-so-cua-lao-dong-tre/206417.vgp.
    [Accessed: 04th Feb, 2015]
14. Hall, E.T. (1981). *Beyond Culture.* Garden City, NY; Doubleday.

15. Haque, M. (2004). *Introduction to Asian public relations*. In D. J. Tilson& E. C. Alozie (Eds.), Toward the common good: Perspectives in international public relations (pp. 341-362). Boston, MA: Pearson Education, Inc.

16. Hang Dinh. (2010). *PR – Ly luan va Ung dung (PR – Theories and Practice)*. Lao Dong – Xa Hoi.

17. Hang Dinh. (2010). *Ngành PR tại Vietnam (PR industry in Vietnam)*. Lao Dong – Xa Hoi.

18. Heath, R. L. (Ed.). (2013). *Encyclopedia of public relations*. Sage.

19. Held, D. (2004) *A Globalizing World? Culture, Economics, Politics*. London: Routledge.

20. Hofstede (1980). *Culture's Consequences*. Beverly Hills, CA: Sage.

21. International Labour Organisation (ILO). (2014). *AEC offers major employment, wage and productivity benefits, if decisively managed*. Retrieved from: http://www.ilo.org/asia/whatwedo/events/WCMS_301202/lang--en/index.htm [Access: 5 Sept 2014]

22. Cornelissen, J. (2009). *Corporate communication: A guide to theory and practice*. Sage.

23. Kvale, S. (1996). Interviews: An introduction to qualitative research interviewing. Thousand Oaks, London: Sage Publications.

24. Le Tran Bao Phuong. (2014). *Quyen Nang Bi An (the Secret Power)*. Information & Communication publisher. Vietnam.

25. LSPR. (2014). *ASEAN PR Network*. Retrieved from: http://lspr.edu/aseanprnetwork/asean-pr-network/ [Access: 5 Sept 2014]

26. McKinney, B. (2008). *An investigation into the perceptions of public relations of Vietnamese business managers. Public Relations Quarterly, 52*, 44-48.

27. Nguyen, Hanh T. (2010). *Exploring public relations practice in Vietnam: public relations functions, practitioners' roles, and most important skills for practitioners*. Ball State University.

28. Nghia Nguyen. (1995). *Methods and techniques of social research (Phươngphápvàkỹthuậttrongnghiêncứuxãhội)*. Open Uninersity HCMC.

29. Paul Holmes. (2010). *Interview with Paul Holmes*. At http://www.forumdavos.com/interviews/read/3 &http://www.youtube.com/watch?v=iYRoHhnoQeo [Accessed: 06 October, 2013]

30. PRSA. (1982). *What is Public Relations (old definition)*. At http://www.prsa.org/AboutPRSA/PublicRelationsDefined/Old%20Definition#.VKJ1TcD 4 [Access: 30 December 2014]

31. PRSA. (2012). *What is Public Relations (modern definition)*. At http://www.prsa.org/AboutPRSA/PublicRelationsDefined/index.html#.VKJ0zcD4 [Access: 30 December 2014]

32. PRSA. (2014). *About us*. At http://www.prsa.org/AboutPRSA/#.VKeY0cmP9f0 [Accessed: 03 January 2015]

33. PR in Malaysia. (2014). About us. At http://iprm.org.my/ [Accessed: 03 January 2015]

34. PR in Singapore. (2014). About us. At http://www.iprs.org.sg/about-us [Accessed: 03 January 2015]

35. PR in Philippine. (2014). About us. At http://www.nationalprcongress.ph/about-prsp/ [Accessed: 03 January 2015]

36. PR in Thailand. (2014). About us. At http://www.prthailand.com/aboutus-en.shtml [Accessed: 03 January 2015]

37. Sriramesh, K. (Ed.) (2004). Public relations in Asia: An anthology. Singapore: Thomson Learning.

38. Sriramesh, K. (2007). *The Relationship between Culture and Public Relations.* In Elizabeth L. Toth (2007), The Future of Excellence in Public Relations and Communication Management, Challenges for the Next Generation, 507-526. Mahwah, NJ: Lawrence Erlbaum Associates, Inc.

39. Sriramesh, K., &Vercic, D. (Eds.). (2003). The global public relations handbook: Theory, research, and practice (pp. 22-37). Routledge.

40. Sriramesh, K., Kim, Y., & Takasaki, M. (1999). *Public relations in three Asian cultures: an analysis.* Journal of Public Relations Research,11(4), 271–292

41. Stacks, D. (2002). *Primer of public relations research.* NY, New York: A Division of Guilford Publications, Inc.

42. Van Leuven, J. K. (1996). *Public relations in South East Asia: From nation building campaigns to regional interdependence.* In H. Culbertson & N. Chen (Eds.), International public relations: A comparative analysis (pp. 207-222). Hillsdale, NJ: Lawrence Erlbaum Associates.

43. Vietnamnews. (2014). *Opportunities abound for PR industry.* Retrieved from http://vietnamnews.vn/economy/258828/opportunities-abound-for-pr-industry.html [Access: 5 Sept 2014]

44. Vietnam+. (2014). *AEC to offer more development opportunities for Vietnam.* Retrieved from http://en.vietnamplus.vn/Home/AEC-to-offer-more-development-opportunities-for-Vietnam/20149/55042.vnplus[Access: 17 Sept 2014]

45. Vita A.D. Busyra. (2014). *PR Community Anticipates Advent of AEC.* Retrieved from http://www.thejakartaglobe.com/international/pr-community-anticipates-advent-aec/[Access: 16 Sept 2014]

46. Wilcox, D.L, Cameron, G.T., Ault, P.H, Agee, W.K. (2003). *Public Relations, Strategies and Tactics*, 7th edition, Allyn and Bacon

47. Wu, M. & Taylor, M. (2003). *Public relations in Taiwan.* Public Relations Review, 29, 473-483.

48. Wu, M. (2005). *Can American public relations theories apply to Asian culture?* Public Relations Quarterly, Fall, 23-27.

49. Wu, M., &Baah-Boakye, K. (2008). *A profile of public relations practice in Ghana.* Public Relations Quarterly, April, 31-36.

50. Wu, M., Taylor, M., & Chen, M. (2001). *Exploring societal and cultural influences on Taiwanese public relations*. Public Relations Review, 27, 317-336.

www.ingramcontent.com/pod-product-compliance
Lightning Source LLC
Chambersburg PA
CBHW070404190526
45169CB00003B/1107